Fariborz Lachini

Golden Autumn 2

Piano Sheet Music

Lachini Media – Canada
http://www.lachini.com

About Fariborz Lachini / Golden Autumn

"Golden Autumn 2" is the second installment in Iranian / Canadian composer/pianist Fariborz Lachini's celebrated series of piano albums called Golden Autumn that includes his original writings for solo piano, some of which were originated from the themes he created for film scores. Lachini has scored for more than a hundred films and is recognized as one of the most innovative composing talents in the Middle East.

Before Iran's Islamic Revolution, Lachini had much success in the pop and music for children fields. After the revolution, he moved to France to study music and computers. Living in Europe influenced Lachini's music into a fusion of contemporary Persian and classical European styles. This blend gives Lachini a unique voice that speaks to Western as well as Middle Eastern sensibilities.

Music Composed and Performed by
Fariborz Lachini
Lachini Media, Canada
http://www.lachini.com

Music Engraved by
David Shenton
NY Music Publishing, USA
http://shentonmusic.com

ISBN-13: 9-781434-829382
ISBN-10: 1434-829383

ISMN: 979-0-706060-01-9
UPC: 634479264320 / Golden Autumn 2 CD

Dance of Leaves

Fariborz Lachini

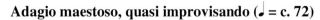

Adagio maestoso, quasi improvisando (♩ = c. 72)

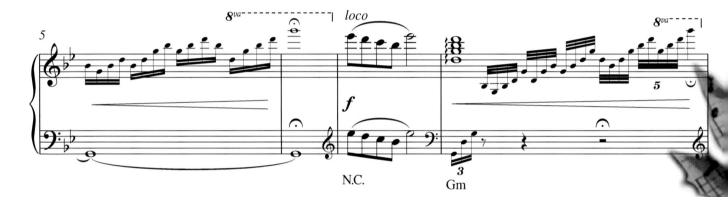

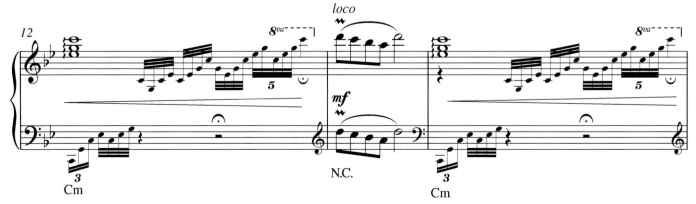

Dance of Leaves

Dance of Leaves

Dance of Leaves

Dance of Leaves

Dance of Leaves

Dance of Leaves

Dance of Leaves

10

9 of 9

Dance of Leaves

Memories of Autumn

Fariborz Lachini

Memories of Autumn

Memories of Autumn

Memories of Autumn

Memories of Autumn

Whirlwind in Autumn

Fariborz Lachini

Whirlwind in Autumn

Whirlwind in Autumn

Whirlwind in Autumn

18

Whirlwind in Autumn

20

Whirlwind in Autumn

Whirlwind in Autumn

Silence of Stars

Fariborz Lachini

Silence of Stars

Silence of Stars

Silence of Stars

Silence of Stars

Loneliness

Fariborz Lachini

Loneliness

Loneliness

28

Loneliness

29

4 of 4

Loneliness

Desire to Stay

Fariborz Lachini

Desire to Stay

Desire to Stay

32

Desire to Stay

Childhood

Fariborz Lachini

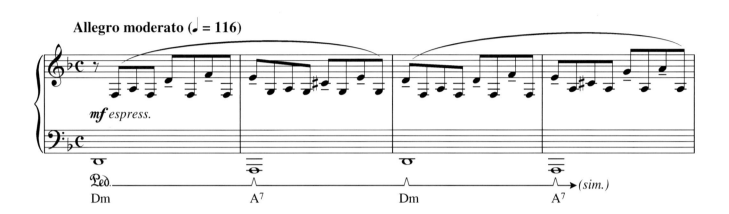

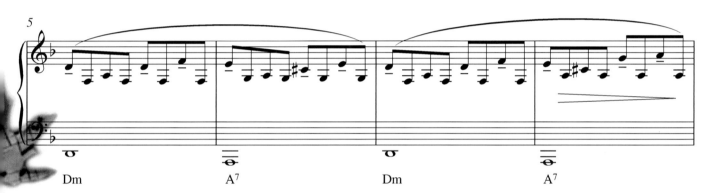

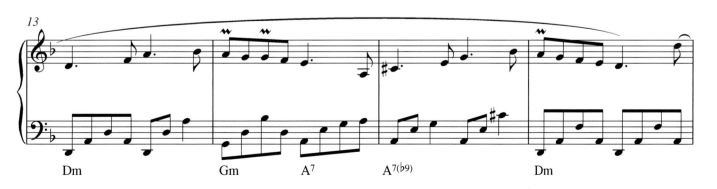

Childhood

Childhood

Childhood

36

I Remember

Fariborz Lachini

I Remember

39

3 of 3

I Remember

Staring in a Mirror

Fariborz Lachini

Staring in a Mirror

Staring in a Mirror

42

Staring in a Mirror

Staring in a Mirror

Stranger

Fariborz Lachini

Stranger

Stranger

46

Stranger

Stranger

Stranger

Trail of Loneliness

Fariborz Lachini

1 of 6   Trail of Loneliness

50

Trail of Loneliness

Trail of Loneliness

Trail of Loneliness

54

What Must Have Been

Fariborz Lachini

What Must Have Been

56

2 of 4

What Must Have Been

3 of 4

What Must Have Been

58

Autumn Slumber

Fariborz Lachini

Autumn Slumber

60

Autumn Slumber

61

3 of 3

Autumn Slumber

Reincarnation

Fariborz Lachini

Reincarnation

Reincarnation

64

Shadow

Fariborz Lachini

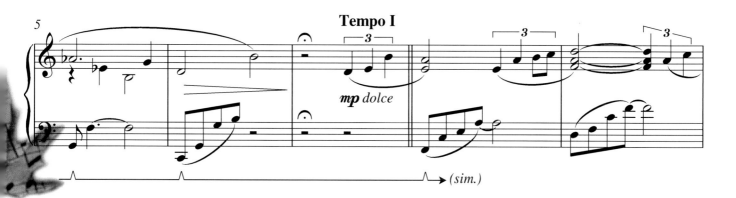

Shadow

Shadow

Shadow

68

Made in the USA
Las Vegas, NV
03 November 2024

11052842R00043